LOVE POEMS AND ELEGIES

By Iain Crichton Smith

IN ENGLISH

Poetry

The Long River
The White Noon (in New Poets, 1959)
Deer on the High Hills
Thistles and Roses
The Law and the Grace
From Bourgeois Land
Selected Poems
Poems to Eimhir by Sorley Maclean (translated)

Literary Criticism

The Golden Lyric (an essay on the poetry of
    Hugh MacDiarmid)

Fiction

Consider the Lilies
The Last Summer
Survival Without Error
My Last Duchess

IN GAELIC

Bùrn is Aran (poems and short stories)
An Dubh is an Gorm (short stories)
Biobuill is Sanasan Reice (poems)
An Coileach (a one-act play)
A'Chùirt (a one-act play)
Iain Am Measg nan Reultan (a children's story)

Love Poems
&
Elegies

IAIN CRICHTON SMITH

LONDON
VICTOR GOLLANCZ LTD
1972

ISBN 0 575 01434 2

PRINTED IN GREAT BRITAIN
BY EBENEZER BAYLIS & SON LIMITED
THE TRINITY PRESS, WORCESTER, AND LONDON

Contents

PART ONE: ELEGIES

PART TWO: POEMS FOR S

Acknowledgements

Of the poems in Part One of this book, numbers 1 to 9 were first published in the magazine *Stand*, Volume 12, No. 2, and numbers 15 to 21 in *Stand*, Volume 12, No. 3.

Part One

ELEGIES

The poems in this part sprang directly from the death of my mother. They lead to reflections on death, on the Highlands, and on particular moments which appeared significant.

You lived in Glasgow

You lived in Glasgow many years ago.
I do not find your breath in the air.
It was, I think, in the long-skirted thirties
when idle men stood at every corner
chewing their fag-ends of a failed culture.
Now I sit here in George Square
where the War Memorial's yellow sword glows bright
and the white stone lions mouth at bus and car.
A maxi-skirted girl strolls slowly by.
I turn and look. It might be you. But no.
Around me there's a 1970 sky.

Everywhere there are statues. Stone remains.
The mottled flesh is transient. On those trams,
invisible now but to the mind, you bore
your groceries home to the 1930 slums.
"There was such warmth," you said. The gaslight hums
and large caped shadows tremble on the stair.
Now everything is brighter. Pale ghosts walk
among the spindly chairs, the birchen trees.
In lights of fiercer voltage you are less
visible than when in winter you
walked, a black figure, through the gaslit blue.

The past's an experience that we cannot share.
Flat-capped Glaswegians and the Music Hall.
Apples and oranges on an open stall.
A day in the country. And the sparkling Clyde
splashing its local sewage at the wall.
This April day shakes memories in a shade

opening and shutting like a parasol.
There is no site for the unshifting dead.
You're buried elsewhere though your flickering soul
is a constant tenant of my tenement.

You were happier here than anywhere, you said.
Such fine good neighbours helping when your child
almost died of croup. Those pleasant Wildes
removed with the fallen rubble have now gone
in the building programme which renews each stone.
I stand in a cleaner city, better fed,
in my diced coat, brown hat, my paler hands
leafing a copy of the latest book.
Dear ghosts, I love you, haunting sunlit winds,
dear happy dented ghosts, dear prodigal folk.

I left you, Glasgow, at the age of two
and so you are my birthplace just the same.
Divided city of the green and blue
I look for her in you, my constant aim
to find a ghost within a close who speaks
in Highland Gaelic.
                              The bulldozer breaks
raw bricks to powder. Boyish workmen hang
like sailors in tall rigging. Buildings sail
into the future. The old songs you sang
fade in their pop songs, scale on dizzying scale.

In your long skirts

In your long skirts among the other girls
you stand beside the barrels, leather-gloved,
in 1908 or so, with severe lips.

The girls are all dead and you are dead.
Two wars have happened since and many fish
have bred and died in the cold North Sea.

In that brown picture you all look very old
for twenty-year-old girls and you're all gazing
to a sun that's off the edge and is made of salt.

You told me once

You told me once how your younger brother died.
It was by drowning. In the tar-black sea
he sang a psalm to bring his rescuers near.
That did not save him though. One cannot hide,
you would have said, from destiny. So here
there are two meanings working side by side.

You died of lack of oxygen. I tried
to fit the mask against your restless face
in the bumpy ambulance in which you lay.
I thought that moment of the psalm as guide
beyond our vain technology, the grey
and scarlet blankets that you tossed aside.

My sailor father

My sailor father died in hospital
of a consumption, forcing you to burn
all your furniture and begin again.
Chair and table blossomed in a hail

of memories which set him in the cordage
of a white schooner setting out to sea,
its sheets unfolding, moving carefully,
the trousseau and red roses of your marriage.

That island formed you

That island formed you, its black hatted men
and stony bibles. How your father's beard
streamed like a cataract. And the heart's devoured
by the black rays of a descending sun.
Always they're making fences, making barred
gates to keep the wind out, their slow pace
deliberate and punctual. Who has heard
of the terrible cyclones that infect deep space?
The daffodils are yellow on the wind
but in these souls where is the love, my dear,
to dally in fine leisure as the clear
smoke rises from the houses, and the cock
shrills redly from the waste abundant air?

The space-ship

I think of you and then I think of this
picture of an astronaut lacking air,
dying of lack of it in the depths of space,

his face kneading and working under glass,
lolling inside his helmet. Then I see
a foreign space-ship steadily from space

swimming implacably, a black helmet
rearing out of the limitless azure and
a sun exploding with tremendous light.

The black mediaeval helmet fits his face
and the glass breaks without a single sound
and becomes the crystals of unnumbered stars.

All our ancestors

All our ancestors have gone abroad.
Their boots have other suns on them. They died
in Canada and Africa with God,

their mouths tasting of exile and of spray.
But you remained. Your grave is in Argyll
among the daffodils beside a tree

feathery and green. A stream runs by,
varying and oral, and your will
becomes a part of it, as the azure sky

trembles within it, not Canadian but
the brilliant sparklings of pure Highland light.

Your brother clanked his sword

Your brother clanked his sword for the Boer War.
Also in Egypt, later still in France.
We won't have much of that continuance.

There'll be no more of that old clattering
among red poppies in a crowded room
of antique ornaments won at Imperial fairs.

Our skies are clearer and more deadly now,
our hell is all around us in the blue
bubble over Hiroshima, our rooms

more pared to their essentials, the chairs
swaying in a purer breeze, the sun
climbing forever to a shriller place.

Those who are needed

Those who are needed do not easily die
or those who think they are needed. When your face
turned to the darkness it was as if the sky
took to itself its light. There were in space
no lightnings from a god. No apples fell.
No new significance present to our slides
keeled from a distant planet and no bell
swung anywhere one could hear. Or if it hides—
some heaven somewhere—with its level blue
and lack of gradient, it's beyond this ship
that through our atmosphere serenely glides
bearing intelligence and anguish too,
its natural pains, the honour that we keep
with ourselves or heaven or our compass guides.

On looking at the dead

This is a coming to reality.
This is the stubborn place. No metaphors swarm

around that fact, around that strangest thing,
that being that was and now no longer is.

This is a coming to a rock in space
worse than a rock (or less), diminished thing

worse and more empty than an empty vase.

The devious mind elaborates its rays.
This is the stubborn thing. It will not move.

It will not travel from our stony gaze.

But it must stay and that's the worst of it
till changed by processes. Otherwise it stays.

To beat against it and no waves of grace
ever to ascend or sovereign price

to be held above it! This is no hero. This
is an ordinary death. If there is grace

theology is distant. Sanctify
(or so they say) whatever really is

and this is real, nothing more real than this.
It beats you down to it, will not permit

the play of imagery, the peacock dance,
the bridal energy or mushrooming crown

or any blossom. It only is itself.
It isn't you. It only is itself.

It is the stubbornness of a real thing

mentionable as such and only such,
the eyes returning nothing. Compromise

is not a meaning of this universe.
And that is good. To face it where it is,

to stand against it in no middle way
but in the very centre where things are

and having it as centre, for you take
directions from it not as from a book

but from this star, black and fixed and here,
a brutal thing where no chimeras are

nor purple colours nor a gleam of silk
nor any embroideries eastern or the rest

but unavoidable beyond your choice
and therefore central and of major price.

Of the uncomplicated dairy girl

Of the uncomplicated dairy girl
in gown that's striped in blue and red
feeding the hens in a windy spring
by the green wooden shed
where shade after quick shade
endlessly shuttles let me speak
and speak unsorrowing.

As in the weather of a Lewis loom
a pastoral picture, striped against the blue,
against the stone, against the green,
against the cottage with its daisies
taking the place of roses
casting the meal from a young hand
still without its ring.

The long dress billows in the breeze
mixed like the confectionery
you'd bring home from the fishing
in the large yellow chest with hats,
silken things and coats,
just before your straight-backed brother
marched off to save the King.

Just stay there therefore for a moment,
uncomplicated dairy girl,
in your chequered screen of red and blue
holding the pail in your hand
before the sky is red and mooned
and feathered by (beyond the dance)
the beat of metal wings.

The burial

The coffin is let down into the grave,
the honey-coloured hexagon's not glass.
I hold a tassel. Past my locked cold face
the little rain goes slanting. It is love

that moves the black sun and the black stars.
It's love that makes my body tremble like
a shorn and meagre ewe when it is struck
by the winds of heaven and it shrinks and cowers.

These verses spoken through the driving rain
do not prevent the coffin's slow descent.
The ribboned wreaths thud on the wood. I stand
confronted by a single vivid scene,

your face in the open coffin, fixed and stern,
rebuker of mortality, incised
to a cold hauteur that I half recognized
as seen on coins or Presbyterian iron.

Tinily a star goes down

Tinily a star goes down
behind a black cloud.

Odd that your wristwatch still should lie
on the shiny dressing table

its tick so faint I cannot hear
the universe at its centre.

The lilies and the daffodils

The lilies and the daffodils shade your face.
They show and do not hide your old bones.
This is your land, this is where you will die,

where the wind blows over and over your hair,
where your dreams sink by inches every year,
where the lilies and daffodils will rise from your bones.

Death and the politicians

The politicians gesture in this bland
and azure summer, superficies
of the mind slumbering in its folded leaves.

None shall speak of the black implacable star
beyond the manifestos of the day
that's unappeased by buttonhole or rose.

As if the floating vote should Charon's boat
guide with its souls to a benignant heaven,
those dim majorities on the other side,

and none shall mention that rotating vase,
constituent of no politics but made
not out of speech but silence and deep shade.

Contrasts

Against your black I set the dainty deer
stepping in mosses and in water where
there are miles of moorland under miles of air.

Against your psalms I set the various seas
slopping against the mussels fixed in place,
slums on the ancient rock in salty rows.

Against your bible I set the plateau
from which I see the people down below
in their random kingdoms moving to and fro.

Against your will I set the changing tones
of water swarming over lucid stones
and salmon bubbling in repeated suns.

Against your death I let the tide come in
with its weight of water and its lack of sin,
the opulent millions of a rising moon.

This clutch of grapes

This clutch of grapes is a clutch of black stars.
Set them against that fine indifferent blue.
Their blackness is a passion of that blue,

their sweetness and their tartness oozing out
in such a taste as hardly we can bear
fattened by an ordinary sun,

a sun so white and common in the sky
which bred this constellation, this swart tribe,
this galaxy of stars so sweet and black,

so round and handsome on their branches where
they seem like globes of death but they are sweet,
the gravities and bells of our desire.

Moonlight over the island

Moonlight over the island, our people gathered
into their black order, into their white,
into the Sundays of the folded hills.

The fishermen walked in Palestine and here
they also walk and in the blue air
black hats like buoys bob churchwards. Also here

the shepherds herd their sheep, and dogs will bark
under such moons explicit as once shone
over the orange groves, the pale sad face

lolling on its cross, while deep below
the crofters slept, and the stones received the moon
in their black mirrors, Palestine or Skye.

The black jar

Exemplar of the exotic with that jar
evolving somewhere in Connecticut

if I shall say I had a jar it would
be a black mountain in the Hebrides

and round it fly your blackbirds black as pitch
and in their centre with a holy book

a woman all in black reading the world
consisting of black crows in a black field.

The chair in which you've sat

The chair in which you've sat's not just a chair
nor the table at which you've eaten just a table
nor the window that you've looked from just a window.
All these have now a patina of your
body and mind, a kind of ghostly glow
which haloes them a little, though invisible.

There is, said Plato, an ideal place
with immortal windows, tables and pure chairs,
archetypes of these, as yet unstained.
In such a world one might look out to space
and see pure roses yet untouched by hand,
the perfect patterns of a universe

of which our furniture is but editions
bred from a printing press which has no end.
The perfect Bible will remain unread
and what we have's a series of translations
which scholars make, each nodding aching head
bowed over texts they never can transcend,

and yet more lovely because truly human,
as tables, chairs and windows in our world
are ours and loved because they taste of us.
Being who we are we must adore the common
copies of perfection, for the grace
of perfect things and angels is too cold.

So in this room I take the luminous
as being the halo of our sweat and love
which makes a chair more than a simple chair,
a table more than a table, dress than dress,
and startlingly striking out of the air
the tigerish access of a crumpled glove.

Argument

He said: We argue and we come to this,
Dostoevsky saying everything is allowed
if there is no continuance after death.
If all the answers have material faces
and no one sees the fine spiritual graces
descending from the heavens in luminous dress
then there's the terror of pure nothingness.

The laws of God engraved on tables were
pure as the morning, for their authorship
was that which made the morning, after all.
The azure and the stone both came together
in a perfected and benignant weather.
The tablets were originals of the air
and made it mean exactly what we are.

If behind the morning there are no
immortal birds parading, if behind
the stubborn stone there isn't more than stone
how shall we find direction? As the hum
of bees in summer harmonises plum
and grape and apple so that these are notes
inside the music which so dominates

the else unmeaning scenery: as in art
the poet knows when he's concluded, for
there's an exactitude that he's aiming at.
He knows it by a sense beyond the poem,
he knows it as he knows a coming home,
perfection to which nothing can be added,
nor by the mind can wholly be decoded.

As even translating from one language to
another one, a residue remains,
there is a gap electricity can't leap.
So words remain ungathered (harvests too)
if that is all that words or harvests do,
that is, just mean themselves, and do not point
to a certain place where both of them are joined.

Everything is allowable, said the Russian,
if death is all there is, if we should stay
fixed to that body, empty as a vase,
which once held life but now is wholly clay,
an object without meaning in our day
of living fish and dogs. That rats should have
their sly quick purpose, their malignant grave

radiance and expression, and you none!
It cannot be that this phenomenon
should disappear as water from a jar.
The world is so impregnated with mind
there must exist a mode at which we find
conversions occurring, like the caterpillars
transformed to moths of an angelic colour.

The Greeks believed the circle was the perfect
figure. Therefore the heavens must conform.
There had to be a way to make ellipses
respectable and so explain the orbit
of planets moving gravely through the light.
It just required a little movement of
a human mind, a justice as of love.

So from a certain stance (as if backstage)
I see the transformation, how the dull
loggish stability becomes the quick
and brilliant foil which lights a whole stage up,
how from a dreary ordinary sleep
lights flash in all directions from pure faces
which are as diamonds in their clear excesses.

Or as in spring an acre becomes blue
and there are bluebells shining mile on mile,
vivid creation of the dullest earth.
Or as in genius ordinary words appear
sngelic, peasant becomes peer,
brown wears the purple, and from hedges flower
whole detonations of remarkable power.

O there are moments when a certain star
rising over the waters is a song,
a glove, a perfume, a remembrancer,
a soul steadily rising, or a "star",
a spiritual Garbo near and far,
a private public being whom the earth
cannot wholly hide though it gave her birth.

I sense a vast connection, spiritual things
bodying forth material, material too
bodying forth the spiritual, so I know
that death is just a place that we have looked
too deeply at, not into, as at a book
held that short space too close. For we must hold
back from a painting so as to see it whole.

And what was blurred becomes quite ordered the:
Out of the chaos marches a whole street
with a church, an inn and houses, people too,
and the light curves all around them with the shape
of a woman in her vulnerable hope
bent over a cradle, tucking sheet and shawl
into an order which is loved and real.

The earth eats everything

The earth eats everything there is.
It is a year and a half now since you died.
Your marble tombstone stands up like a book.
The storms have not read it nor the leaves.
The blue lightnings bounced from it.
The ignorant swallows perched on its top.
I have forgotten it over and over.
Life is explainable only by life.
I have read that on paper leaves.

Part Two

POEMS FOR S

No one at home

There is never anyone at home when I call.
Through the wrought railings I can see your study
through the pale window but you're never at home.
I leave your house and walk the street again.
They are hooking men at the open air draughtsboard
and I hear soft music playing in the Gardens.
The mind has terrifying labyrinths.
"Wherever you wander, O wherever you roam
there is no place as terrible as home."
Restless you prowl the streets, your learning lodged
with the snakes of your brain's attics. I remember
you standing with a cocktail in your hand.
You were as white as an eel I saw once,
upright in the water, almost dead.
It was an angel of the endless waste.
You are an angel whose bubbles are all gone.
Your thousands of books waterfall the walls.
You pressed a name and a bell would once ring.
Now there are no bells: you've pulled the wires.
The citizens walk their dogs in the evening,
their bell-shaped faces ruminant and red.
They do not know enough to be so tired.

I thought I saw you

I thought I saw you on the street just now
in your biscuit-coloured slacks. It wasn't you.
Nothing will ever die, not even lies.
The taxi's meter clicked. There was a view
of Glasgow's ruinous land of green and blue.
When will the heart learn better enterprise?

Hotels receive me. What receives your ghost?
What elevator, station, road or slum?
The mind has tricks that we are desperate for.
How can we turn away? There is no home
other than it, and where you go or come
is here or elsewhere but is always here.

Resurrection

You rise from the dead ghosts of last night's party
combing your hair, a Venus from the blue
scarred flowing ashtrays. It is almost due,
the hour of transformation, when the sky

receives you, combed and lipsticked once again,
rouged for the morning, perfect to your scale.
Slowly your face brightens, slowly you sail
at another prow of morning towards noon.

The world's a minefield

The world's a minefield when I think of you.
I must walk carefully in case I touch
some irretrievable and secret switch
that blows the old world back into the new.

How careless I once was about this ground
with the negligence of ignorance. Now I take
the smallest delicate steps and now I look
about me and about me without end.

Do not put on that wig

Do not put on that wig. Be what you are.
The tranquilliser, Caesar's constant star,
is not enough. We would go through it all,
helmeted with the pure and hammered will,
though Floddens still roar round us. Do not paint
that grey hair out. You'll hear me still indignant
under the flag, under the fading shield,
though the black shapes go stabbing round the field

What tragedy is

What tragedy is is to hope for the one thing forever.
(Comedy is not forever. It is only for a short time.
It is the play of a summer's day.)

But O the shadow that falls steadily in the one spot,
so loyal to the ground, such an old retainer,
bowing lower and lower under the weight of itself.

The trees and you

If it were that the trees would ripen with fruit
steadily, extravagantly, without concentration.

If it were that we need not think them into being,
the consistent plenitude of the apples.

If it were that we were innocent of all contriving,
that I need not phone each moment to find out how you are.

Sleepless

Sleepless in one room thinking of another room,
of the old helmets moulding the bone to themselves,

of the light clamped in the ceiling looking down
with the indifference of your early days, shaping your head
   to the pillow.

Youth and Age

In youth engagements are not perilous
only in themselves not for the two.

In age the care is doubly precious
not to be alone in the night
and to walk carefully about the days.

Love, if you are love

Love, if you are love why do you fail?
I thought a constant shining would be enough
for even the moon makes ruins beautiful.
But love is not a miracle maker.
                              So
a phone can ring but sometimes it does not.
The heart may lightly tremble for its ring
whose harsh sonority unsinews it.

I think we are both sick

I think we are both sick.
When our heads touch they seem to scorch each other.
Our lips are drinking each other's ruin,

quietly just quietly breathing in unison.
Your eyes are wedged open, staring at me
just like a badger's frightened in the dark.

The place without music

Look steadily at the place without music
for you will come to it, some day you will come.
To clench the teeth is only one device.
Another is to leaf through early days
with patience before large busy windows.
There are some others but the best of all
is to remember it is natural,
to outstare it steadily as a child does
neither with shame nor yet with penitence.

The fever

Our heads burn together but our hands are cold.
In ruinous excess to go out into the night
was left to Romeo and Juliet.

For our part we burn with a steady fever,
separate though together, the heat that comes from each
not quite enough to make the one star.

In the cinema

You rest your head on my shoulder. Wellington says:
"Blücher must come soon. He must come soon."
It is raining steadily on the cinema roof.

Slowly I see the Prussians in black armour
rising above your head. Moustaches writhe.
Your hair is in my nostrils. You have fallen asleep.

The bouquet

You brought me a bouquet, salt with brine.
Neither was it your fault. The sea is salt.

The sea is darker than anyone dares to know.
The lights more bright for vaster distances.

Inside the poem

All night I have been writing.
I have taken you into my poems.

You can walk about in them quite naturally.
You can put your hair up if you like,
you can lift your stockinged legs on to the bed.

Dearest, there is plenty of space.
I will not hammer the walls too close.
I shall leave plenty of silences.

You can sit in front of a mirror on a chair,
and make the poem look back at you.
It is all the same. Only one thing:
don't draw the curtains for I wish to look at you.

On the train

Nothing is cool and green any more.
My brain could burn that ashtray where it stands
on the table that this train is carrying north.
Outside there is a greenness and big stones,
hills that go on forever, brawling streams.
But the rails are heating, they converge on something.
Logic has failed us. We are burning up.
The adored days are bowed on other lakes.

Guilts

Your father played a piano made of bone.
You took your teddy bear to sleep with you.
Nothing can hide our guilt and nothing can
stop the unnecessary deaths from rising.
So that is why you send your money to
refugees, black, unrecognisable . . .
asking forgiveness of their poverty.
There are so many . . . Not teddy bears enough
to make them sleep nor Beethoven enough
to make the flesh arise upon their bones.

In the hotel

In the hotel a wash basin and a mirror.
The street outside is brown with fallen leaves.

I sit with hanging arms like a tired boxer
under the light of your one aching bulb.

The dream

I tremble like a needle on a compass.
The space between us is a No Man's Land.
Somewhere to the east the sun is rising
and to the west is setting . . . There is no
romance in our natures, only a safe keeping.
I dream a dream. With a green ring in my hand
I'm drifting towards you, we are great moon bears
hulking in light. And then you drift away.
Hiking my oxygen I follow you.
And then I am alone. The space-ship's gone.
You're at the window, white face peering out.
The taxi streams in rain past a green star.

Night

Night and we are drinking yet again,
all of us. The stars in the autumn sky
are eaten by the blackness as a dog
mercilessly crunches some white bones.

We walk along a street of absences,
kiosks, pillar boxes, all official red
with bangles of white dew, and the lamps
globular and high and whisky coloured.

We hold each other's hands. Ah, Racine,
with your crystal kings and queens, your perfect classic
mechanisms of tragedy and power.
In your Roman study what would you think of us?

Or you Paul Valery whose philosophy
is a calm roof of water where the tombs
engraved with doves and angels interrupt
eloquent summers brutal with desire.

I put my hand in yours, a mortal chain.
Under the thin cloth your body ripens.
It is composed of towers and apples and
secrecies and absences and moons.

Racine's imperial verse is wholly gone.
We stand together by a gate in autumn
with your unbruised helmet and a pair
of fine red gloves held loosely in your hands.

Where are you tonight?

Where are you tonight as the rain falls?
Are you reading interminably in your room
as a child does in the shadow and the flame?
Remember that game that we played together
on another day of wet dark weather
naming in the bookshops all the books we'd read.
I hadn't read Du Maurier nor you Ballard.
We are not the kind who can ski or ride.
Sometime long ago we were sent to bed
and held the page up like a tombstone
which later was our fascination and our pride.
To communicate in quotations . . . Some do that,
as if they were facsimiles of other men's thoughts,
footnotes explainable by scholarship.
We are like asterisks in the shady sky
and more translatable than poetry.
I see you bowed in the rain over
your green and humming leaves forever
child, reader, insatiable sister,
phantom of a book, holding a book in your hands.

At the Scott Exhibition, Edinburgh Festival

(I)

He will outlast us, churning out his books,
advocate and historian, his prose
earning him Abbotsford with its borrowed gates,
its cheap mementos from the land he made.
Walking the room together in this merciless
galaxy of manuscripts and notes
I am exhausted by such energy.
I hold your hand for guidance. Over your brow
the green light falls from tall and narrow windows.
His style is ignorant of this tenderness,
the vulnerable angle of your body
below the Raeburn with its steady gaze.

(II)

It was all in his life, not in his books
"Oh I am dying, take me home to Scotland
where I can breathe though that breath were my last."
He limped through an Edinburgh being made anew.
He worked his way through debts, past a dead wife.
My dear, we love each other in our weakness
as he with white grave face diminishing through
stroke after stroke down to the unpaid room.
We know what we are but know not what we will be.
I tremble in this factory of books.
What love he must have lost to write so much.